50 MUSICAL ACTIVITIES FOR CHILDREN

50 Musical Activities for Children

ALISON HEDGER

with cartoons by
JO HEDGER

EASTBOURNE

Copyright © 2001 Alison Hedger

The right of Alison Hedger to be identified
as author of this work has been asserted by her in
accordance with the Copyright, Designs
and Patents Act 1988.

First published 2001

All rights reserved.
No part of this publication may be reproduced or
transmitted in any form or by any means, electronic
or mechanical, including photocopy, recording, or any
information storage and retrieval system, without
permission in writing from the publisher.

ISBN 0 85476 935 8

Published by
KINGSWAY PUBLICATIONS
Lottbridge Drove, Eastbourne, BN23 6NT, England.
Email: books@kingsway.co.uk

Book design and production for the publishers by
Bookprint Creative Services, P.O. Box 827, BN21 3YJ, England.
Printed in Great Britain.

Contents

Introduction   9
How to Use This Book   11

Section 1. Knowing God – Father, Son and Holy Spirit

1. Father in Heaven   17
2. Point, Clap and Say   20
3. My Eyes Have Seen the Glory of the Lord   22
4. On the Pulse   26
5. Be Still and Know That I Am God   28
6. Kieran's Bicycle   32
7. Stick Clicks and a Bong!   34
8. Three in One   36
9. Triple Layering   38
10. Jesus Will Be the Same Today   40
11. High, Wide and Deep   43
12. Nothing Can Separate Us from God's Love   45
13. Word Colouring   47
14. Love the Lord With All of Your Heart   50
15. Step in Time   54
16. Pass the Drum   55
17. Jesus Loves Me   56
18. Word Play   60
19. Play a Pan!   61

50 MUSICAL ACTIVITIES FOR CHILDREN

20.	Take All Your Troubles to Jesus	62
21.	Move Along	64
22.	Circle Fun	66
23.	Blow the Trumpet, Bang the Drum	68
24.	Big Band March	71

Section 2. How to Live

25.	Equipping a Child for Life	74
26.	Pulse and Rhythm	79
27.	Be Not Overcome with Evil	81
28.	Good Triumphs over Evil	84
29.	Conversation	86
30.	The People of God's Church Are One Body	87
31.	Shakers and Tube Trumpets	92
32.	Blowing Bottles	93
33.	Greed in the End Is No Friend	94
34.	Hitting the Right Pitch	98
35.	The Gardener Sows His Seed	99
36.	Mirror Images	104
37.	Growing Plants	105
38.	Scatter Seeds of Good Today	106
39.	Heel and Toe	110
40.	Don't Be a Copycat of Things That Are Bad	111
41.	Follow My Sticks	116
42.	Copy My Guiro Rhythm	117
43.	Gently Rock	118
44.	Sharing Favourite Toys	121
45.	Out of the Boat	123
46.	Humpty-Dumpty Was a Duff Egg	125
47.	Smash!	128
48.	Mugs and Cups	129
49.	Little Bo-Peep Had Silly Sheep	131
50.	Shepherd's Name-calling Game	133

CONTENTS

Index of Themes	135
Resources	137
CD Track List	139

Introduction

My hope is that this book will help, inspire and strengthen our work with children, using God's wonderful gift of music, bringing deeper faith and understanding to all involved in children's ministry, as well as their children, families and friends.

Music is fun – the children's own enthusiasm and inventiveness will make these activities something to look forward to, and to reflect upon afterwards. Biblical truths conveyed through the medium of music are quickly learned and easily remembered. The close link in the human memory between a tune and its lyrics is a wonderful attribute given to us, and can be used at any time, anywhere. Children may forget lots of facts, but those linked to a melody or activity will long be remembered.

'Dear Lord, we thank you for the joy of music, and for making it something in which we can all share. Music holds people together in a very special way and is a wonderful gift. Thank you. Amen.'

How to Use This Book

The book contains 20 original songs and 30 musical-related activities, and falls into two main sections:

1. Knowing God – Father, Son and Holy Spirit
2. How to live

Every song has a biblical focus, and all the songs are short and easy to learn. I have included some helpful Scripture references and written some children's prayers, but you may prefer to source your own biblical texts and write your own prayers. At least one related musical activity is given for each song, and these range from actions to the use of school-type percussion instruments, and playing rhythm sticks, and games.

Use is also made of musical devices which children will be familiar with from their music lessons at school – rounds, ostinati, timbre and layering of sounds. Please do not be put off if this book sounds too ambitious or you think you are tone deaf! Everyone can enjoy this collection of songs and activities. You don't need to be a trained musician – just be enthusiastic!

The CD will be invaluable, and is a great resource in itself. It has each song clearly sung for ease of learning, as well as the backing tracks without vocals for children to sing along to. In some cases the backing tracks are also for use with a musical activity, and of course you can programme your player to repeat the music just as many times as you need. Each song is written out as a simple piano part, and is suitable for the average player at Sunday school and at home. But if you are an able keyboard player, you may wish to fill out the accompaniments, as you feel able.

Please embellish the music as suits your needs, using appropriate musical instruments and drum kit as available. Chord symbols are given, and the lyrics for each song are clearly set out. Some of the songs and activities are intended for use with very young children, although you will probably find everyone will want to have fun with these too! Most songs and activities are suitable for mixed ages and abilities, and could be useful for all-age worship or church family parties.

A few musical terms explained

Tempo: the speed of a piece of music. This is traditionally indicated by a metronome mark at the beginning of the written music, giving the speed of the beats, thus: ♩ = 120

Beat or pulse: the throbbing of the music, which carries it along in a regular fashion.

Rhythm: the sound pattern, or placing of the notes with accents and stresses. It does not refer to the melody, although of course a tune will have a rhythm to it, otherwise every note would be of equal length (very boring!).

Pitch: this refers to where the notes are melodically, and has nothing to do with how long or short, loud or soft the notes are. The notes could be high, low or in the middle. When everyone is on the same note (at the same pitch) we say it is 'in tune'.

Ostinato: a recurring pattern fitting in with a piece of music. This can be melodic (a tune) or it can be purely rhythmic (no melody).

Round: a song where two or more parts begin the same melody, but at different times. All the parts fit together to make a simple tune sound quite complicated.

Help with percussion instruments

Percussion instruments are struck to make the sound. A wide selection of percussion, based on ethnic instruments from around the world, is available from school stockists, and these instruments are especially appropriate for use at all stages of children's development. Percussion instruments are made in a variety of materials and each has its own sound characteristics – wood, metal, plastic, etc. The sound of an instrument is varied by using a hard, medium or soft beater. It is wise to convey to children that playing percussion is not synonymous with playing as loudly as possible! Try to develop some sensitivity and produce appropriate sounds for the task in hand. Many times, the best effects are obtained by playing quietly.

School percussion instruments tend to be rather expensive, but many exciting sounds can be created by recycled packaging or kitchen utensils. Tap each pot, pan, mug and container using wooden, plastic and metal spoons. Investigate packaging before you throw it away. Are there corrugated ridges that could be stroked with a pencil, to make the sound of a guiro? Stretch elastic bands and twang them; blow empty bottles to see if they make the sound you are looking for; blow thin paper over a comb; wave sheets of paper and card to make the sound of wobble boards. A bunch of keys makes a delightful sound, and don't forget saucepan lids as cymbals.

Cling film stretched over an empty plastic bowl makes an

excellent drum, especially for finger sounds. Shakers made by filling empty plastic bottles (many with ideal hand-holds for young children) are easy to make and the sound produced differs according to what you fill them with. Investigate using pebbles, lentils, rice and marbles. Crinkle up crisp packets, twang egg slicers and play upturned empty biscuit tins as drums. Once you get into search mode in the kitchen and by the bin, you will discover sounds and ideas of your own.

The proper name for rhythm sticks is claves (originally from Cuba) which are 18 cm hardwood rounded sticks, played by tapping them together. Rhythm sticks can also be played at floor level by tapping on the floor. They can be made cheaply at home by purchasing 2 cm dowel and cutting it into equal, pencil length pieces. Sand off any rough areas and either leave them as natural wood or decorate them as you choose.

Have fun!

Section 1

Knowing God –
Father, Son and Holy Spirit

1. Father in Heaven

Biblical reference

Matthew 6:9–13

Prayer

The Lord's Prayer

Song words

Father in heaven you are Lord over all,
special and holy is your name.
Your kingdom come,
and your will it must be done
on this earth, as it is done in heaven.
Give us this day our daily bread,
and help us to forgive like you do.
Lead us away from everything that is bad,
giving you the glory and the power.

FATHER IN HEAVEN

FATHER IN HEAVEN

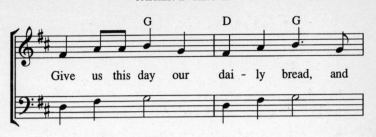

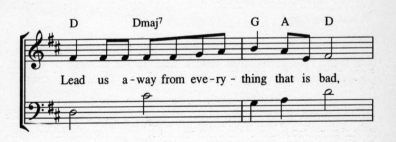
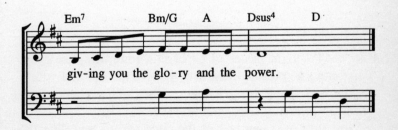

2. Point, Clap and Say

Biblical reference

1 Timothy 6:14–15

What you need

Eight sheets of A4 paper or card. On one side of each sheet is the word 'King' in large letters, and on the reverse of each sheet is the word 'Jesus'.

The word 'King' is one clap = ♩ (a crotchet)

The word 'Jesus' has two claps = ♫ (quavers)

What you do

Lay out the eight pieces of paper in a row, 'King' side up. Point at each sheet and say, in a positive manner and with a regular beat, 'King, King, King. . .'. The children clap and say 'King' with you.

Now turn over any one of the eight sheets, revealing the word 'Jesus'. Point and say with the children clapping as before, but now one of the eight words will be 'Jesus', which has two claps. Turn over a second sheet, and now two of the words will be 'Jesus'.

Invite a child to turn the sheets over as he or she wishes, perhaps turning back the 'Jesus' sheets to 'King' sheets. The children will be eager to have a go. Once you have the hang of this, you can assign a child to be the leader and do the pointing.

3. My Eyes Have Seen the Glory of the Lord

Biblical references

Psalm 148

Genesis 1 and 2:1–3

Prayer

Dear God, you made the world and everything in it. Let our eyes see your glory in all the things around us. Give us a big heart to say 'thank you' for creating such a fantastic world for us to live in. Help us to treat your creation with care, so that everything good you have made can be enjoyed by those who will come after us. Amen.

Order of God's creation

Day one   Light

Day two   Separation of waters into sky above and water below

MY EYES HAVE SEEN THE GLORY OF THE LORD

Day three   Land, sea, grass and trees

Day four   Sun, moon, stars, seasons and time

Day five   Fish and birds

Day six   Animals and man (male and female) in the image of God. Ordered man to be master of fish, birds and animals.

Day seven   Holy rest

Song words

1. My eyes have seen the glory of the Lord
   In every single thing that he has made.
   He gave us perfect light
   So that day-time was not night.
   Yes! My eyes have seen the glory of the Lord.

2. My eyes have seen the glory of the Lord
   In every single thing that he has made.
   He laid out way up high,
   An expanse that we call sky.
   Yes! My eyes have seen the glory of the Lord.

3. My eyes have seen the glory of the Lord
   In every single thing that he has made.
   He made the sea and land,
   And all plants, by his own hand.
   Yes! My eyes have seen the glory of the Lord.

4. My eyes have seen the glory of the Lord
   In every single thing that he has made.
   The sun and moon enhanced
   By a million stars that dance.
   Yes! My eyes have seen the glory of the Lord.

5. My eyes have seen the glory of the Lord
   In every single thing that he has made.
   His creatures of the sky
   And the sea, can swim and fly.
   Yes! My eyes have seen the glory of the Lord.

6. My eyes have seen the glory of the Lord
   In every single thing that he has made.
   The animals galore,
   And his people to adore!
   Yes! My eyes have seen the glory of the Lord.

7. My eyes have seen the glory of the Lord
   In every single thing that he has made.
   God took a holy rest,
   And day seven he then blessed.
   Yes! My eyes have seen the glory of the Lord.

8. So let creation make a merry noise
   And sing to God with thankfulness and joy.
   God's world is very good
   So we'll treat it as we should.
   Yes! My eyes have seen the glory of the Lord.

MY EYES HAVE SEEN THE GLORY OF THE LORD

All the verses use the identical rhythm as given for verse one.

4. On the Pulse

Biblical reference

Genesis 1:31

What you need

Someone to bang a drum and keep a steady pulse if you are unsure of your own regular beats.

What you do

Clap eight recurring beats and chant the following words as shown:

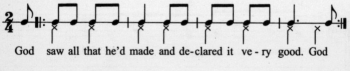

God saw all that he'd made and de-clared it ve - ry good. God

(⤫ = the eight recurring beats)

Add simple actions in time to the beats:

ON THE PULSE

(a) Two knee taps and two hand claps

(b) One head tap, one shoulder tap, two hand claps

Ask the children to make up their own action patterns, but keep them very simple and in time to the beats.

5. Be Still and Know That I Am God

Biblical references

Psalm 121:7

Psalm 46:1–3

Psalm 91:1–6

Matthew 24:1–35

Prayer

Dear Lord, help us not to panic whatever happens. Help us to stay calm and to know that you are right there beside us. Amen.

Song words

1. Be still and know that I am God.
   Do not fear for I am near.
   Be still and know that I am God.
   If mountains quake and all things shake,
   If seas foam, you're not alone.
   Be still and know that I am God.

2. Be still and know that I am God.
   Do not fear for I am near.
   Be still and know that I am God.
   If earth and heaven fall apart,
   Don't be afraid, keep me in your heart.
   Be still and know that I am God.

3. Be still and know that I am God.
   Do not fear for I am near.
   Be still and know that I am God.
   If all you know should pass away,
   Don't despair, you'll hear me say,
   'Be still and know that I am God.'

BE STILL AND KNOW THAT I AM GOD

6. Kieran's Bicycle

What you need

Percussion instruments and everyday items to illustrate the following story. It would be an idea to read the story without any sound colouring, before allowing the children to try out instruments for themselves and see if they make an appropriate sound.

What you do

Add sound colour to the story at the places marked with an asterisk. Some suggestions are given.

(a) Kieran had a beautiful new bicycle for his birthday.*
    (Use a swooshing sound made with fingers circling on a drum to represent the wheel noise, and perhaps a cycle bell.)

(b) Imagine how Kieran felt, when one day he discovered that some bullies had taken the back wheel off his bike, and thrown the bolts away.*
    (Use sounds to represent sadness growing into anger,

KIERAN'S BICYCLE

triggered off by a bolt being dropped into a metal tin. Sound can get to a furious level and stop abruptly, perhaps by a clash on a cymbal.)

(c) The still small voice of God stopped Kieran in his tracks.*
(Try a single ting on a triangle followed by silence.)

(d) 'I am with you,' said God. 'I will help you with your anger and disappointment.'*
(Try warm and comforting sounds.)

(e) Just then Kieran's Uncle Bill, the car mechanic, happened to pass by. 'Hello, Kieran. I just happened to be passing and I wondered how you were,' said Uncle Bill. 'Have you got anything for me to fix? You know how I love mending things and putting them together again.'*
(Use sounds of nuts and bolts, hammering, scraping, etc.)

(f) Kieran showed Uncle Bill his sad-looking bicycle without the wheel. Uncle Bill got to work, and in next to no time it was mended. Uncle Bill had just the right bolts inside his overalls. The bicycle was as good as new.
(Bicycle sounds as before.)

(g) Kieran thanked Uncle Bill for his help, and he thanked God for saving him from his anger and disappointment, and for making everything all right. In fact he felt so happy that he sang his favourite song.*
(The children sing their favourite song together to an accompaniment played on the things used to colour the story.)

7. Stick Clicks and a Bong!

Biblical reference

Psalm 124:8

What you need

Rhythm sticks (see 'How to Use This Book'). If these are not available, use hand claps instead.

What you do

Children sit in a circle on the floor and chant the words to the following rhythm.

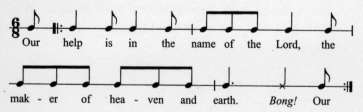

Use the rhythm sticks to keep a steady beat, or play with the words to make a rhythm. Add in a fun noise for the final 'Bong!'.

8. Three in One

Biblical reference

Matthew 28:19

Prayer

Dear God, you are God alone. We praise you as our Maker, as our Saviour, Jesus Christ and as the Holy Spirit who leads us into all truth. Amen.

Song words

> Our heavenly Father is one God
> And Jesus is his Son.
> The Holy Spirit is God's power,
> And all are three in One.

THREE IN ONE

9. Triple Layering

What you need

Three groups of different sounding percussion instruments. Perhaps a group of drums, a group of guiros and a group of tambourines would work well. See 'How to Use This Book' for instrument ideas.

What you do

Sit the children with their instruments in three groups.

Group one plays a steady beat:

♩   ♩
One   God

The second group plays:

♫   ♩
Je - sus   Christ

TRIPLE LAYERING

The third group plays:

Ho - ly Spi - rit

Practise each group separately, then begin layering the sound by adding the groups in one at a time. Play the backing track to the song 'Three in One', and play along with this. The leader's instructions directing which group may play at any one time must be obeyed!

To make an alternative bit of fun, ask all the players to play just on the 'pom-pom', as marked in the music. Very young children will enjoy this (as will all grown ups!) and you could augment your sound layering with this part.

10. Jesus Will Be the Same Today

Biblical reference

Hebrews 13:8

Prayer

Dear Lord Jesus, technology is rapidly changing our lives. Help us to stop for a moment, and to hear your peaceful voice in our hearts. You are the same today as you were yesterday, and tomorrow you will still be the same Jesus. We need to know this and never to be afraid of change, because in you we have someone really special who never changes. You are always just the same. Amen.

Song words

Part one

    Jesus will be the same today
    As he will be tomorrow.
    Jesus has always been the same,
    The Son of God.

Part two

    Jesus Christ the Son of God.
    Jesus Christ the Son of God.

JESUS WILL BE THE SAME TODAY
(two parts)

Only attempt singing the two parts together once the children are able to sing the song all the way through with confidence.

11. High, Wide and Deep

Biblical reference

Ephesians 3:18

What you need

Four distinctive sounds: for example, percussion instruments (or anything else to hand, such as clashing saucepan lids), two shoes to bang together, a whistle, and a bendy ruler to twang against a table. Four people to make the sounds.

What you do

Each sound acts as a cue for a particular action by the children to illustrate the four words:

Wide = arms and legs stretched out sideways
Long = right arm and leg stretched to front, and left arm and leg stretched out backwards
High = stretch up tall as possible on tiptoes
Deep = crouch down with hands on the floor

Practise co-ordinating the actions with the sounds. When they are well co-ordinated (get to the position when no vocal prompt is needed, and the children are responding just to the sound cue) jumble the order of the sounds and try and catch the children out!

12. Nothing Can Separate Us from God's Love

Biblical reference

Romans 8:38–39

Prayer

Father God, as we pray, let your love fill us. Nothing can ever separate us from you, however bad things get. This is a really special love and something which we treasure. Amen.

Song words (to be sung as a round)

> Nothing can separate us from God's love,
> From God's love, from God's love.
> This is very good to know.

NOTHING CAN SEPARATE US FROM GOD'S LOVE
(a round)

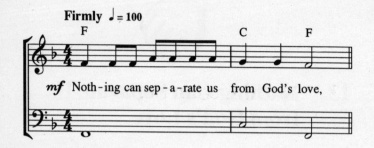
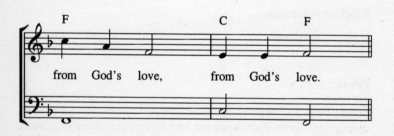
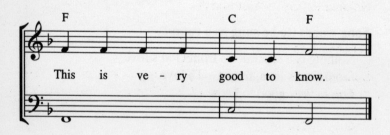

It would be best not to attempt the song as a round until the children are singing with confidence.

13. Word Colouring

Biblical references

John 4:1–15

Matthew 10:42

What you need

Three different sounds – perhaps a tambourine, a single suspended cymbal with a soft beater and a woodblock – or use everyday items (see 'How to Use This Book'). Three children to play the instruments.

What you do

Read the following story. Then assign one of the three instruments to a particular word, as follows:

Sun = tambourine
Hot = cymbal
Drink = woodblock

Re-read the story and every time the key words are read, the designated instrument plays. Gradually speed up the reading as you repeat the story. The children will become familiar with what is coming next. Remember to let other children also have a turn. Then, in order to trick the children into perhaps anticipating their word because they are not really listening to the story, read the second version, but don't warn the children you are changing the story!

Version one

The sun shone. The sun shone and it was very hot. It was so hot that Mandy couldn't sit in the sun any longer. She went inside to get a drink. 'Are you too hot, dear?' asked her mum. 'Here, drink this cool clear water.' 'Thanks, Mum.' When Mandy had finished her drink and she wasn't so hot, she went outside again into the sun.

Version two

The sun shone. The fun had gone out of the day as it was so very hot. It wasn't that Mandy wouldn't sit outside any longer, but the sun was making her thirsty. She went inside. Mum asked her, 'Are you too hot, dear? Here, have a lollipop.' 'I'd rather have some water, thanks, Mum,' said Mandy. Mandy went outside once more into the sun and she took another drink of water with her, just in case she got hot again.

14. Love the Lord With All of Your Heart

Biblical references

Deuteronomy 6:4–5

Leviticus 19:18

Mark 12:28–31

Prayer

Dear Jesus, you have asked us to love God with our feelings and to love him from the depths of our being. You want us to love God in our thinking and with all our effort. This is your first rule. The second is to do to other people what we would like them to do to us. In this way we shall be treating everyone as you mean us to. Please help us to keep your two great commandments. Amen.

LOVE THE LORD WITH ALL OF YOUR HEART

Song words

Love the Lord with all of your heart
And with all your soul.
Love the Lord with all of your mind
And with all of your strength.

God is One and Lord of us all.
This we know is true.
Love your neighbour as yourself,
Is what he tells us to do.

Love the Lord with all of your heart
And with all your soul.
Love the Lord with all of your mind
And with all of your strength.

LOVE THE LORD
WITH ALL OF YOUR HEART

LOVE THE LORD WITH ALL OF YOUR HEART

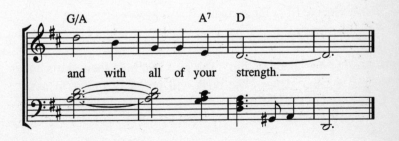

15. Step in Time

What you need

A large empty space and the accompanying CD to this book playing the backing music to the song 'Love the Lord with all of your heart'.

What you do

Step in time to the three beats using three equal little steps. The speed is quite quick but the recording makes the three counts quite obvious:

1 2 3 / 1 2 3 / 1 2 3 etc.

Now change from three equal little steps to:

dip-step-step/ dip-step-step

Bend at the knee for 'dip'. The girls can hold their skirts and twirl as they dance. The boys will probably prefer to have their hands straight by their sides, as is the fashion of Irish country dancing.

16. Pass the Drum

What you need

A hand drum or a home-made finger drum. No beater is needed.

What you do

Sit in a circle on the floor and clap the rhythm of the first words of the song 'Love the Lord with all of your heart'.

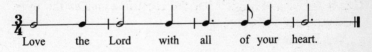

When this rhythm is secure, chant the words very quietly. One person has the drum and plays along with the words. During the next 'Love the Lord with all of your heart' the drum is passed to the next person in the circle, who then beats the subsequent 'Love the Lord with all of your heart'. This way, there is the drum playing alternating with the quiet chant, which gives young children time to pass the drum on. If you are working with a large number of children, use two or three different sounding instruments, spacing them equally around the circle.

17. Jesus Loves Me

Biblical reference

Mark 10:13–16

Prayer

Thank you, Lord Jesus, for loving every little child. Amen.

Song words

1. Jesus loves me, (three times)
   Yes, he does.
   Jesus loves me, (twice)
   Keeping me in his great love.

2. Jesus loves you, (three times)
   Yes, he does.
   Jesus loves you, (twice)
   Keeping you in his great love.

3. Jesus loves all the little children,
   Jesus loves them,
   Yes, he does.
   Jesus loves all the little children,
   Keeping them in his great love.

Actions

These are very simple.

Point to yourself on 'me'.

Point to others on 'you'.

Spread arms wide on 'all the little children'.

Fold arms across chest on 'keeping me in his great love'.

JESUS LOVES ME
(actions)

JESUS LOVES ME

18. Word Play

What you need

All the children to know the words of the first verse of the song 'Jesus loves me'.

What you do

(a) Gently clap the words as you whisper them (just tiny tapping, not full hand claps). Have a gentle tap for each syllable.

(b) Repeat as for (a), but suddenly have two very loud claps and voice at full volume for 'great love'.

(c) Repeat (a), but start slowly and get quicker and quicker. Do not get louder and louder, just quicker and quicker. Keep a whispering voice throughout.

(d) Begin as for (a) but gradually get louder and louder. Do not get quicker and quicker, just louder and louder at the same speed.

You will need a good leader for this activity as all the children must keep together!

19. Play a Pan!

What you need

Hang an assortment of pots and pans on a broom handle slung between two chair backs. Have ready a variety of wooden and metal spoons for playing the pans.

What you do

Sing the song 'Jesus loves me'. Designate a particular word when the pans must be struck:

(a) 'me' = one bang

(b) 'Jesus' = two bangs

(c) 'yes, he does' = three bangs

(d) 'little children' = four bangs

Depending upon the variety of pans and assortment of children, you could have a saucepan orchestra and have (a), (b), (c) and (d) all playing, perhaps to the CD recording, so that they all keep together.

20. Take All Your Troubles to Jesus

Biblical references

Matthew 6:25–34

Matthew 11:28

Prayer

Dear Jesus, no trouble is too big or too small to bring to you in prayer. No worry is too odd or awful for us to share with you. Help us to know the special care you have for each and every one of us. May we leave all our troubles and worries with you. Amen.

Song words

> Take all your troubles to Jesus,
> Leave all your worries behind.
> Trust in the love of Jesus Christ –
> Wonderful peace you will find.

TAKE ALL YOUR TROUBLES TO JESUS

Wave goodbye to partner on words 'Bye-bye'.

21. Move Along

What you need

A large clear space and the backing track for the song 'Take all your troubles to Jesus', programmed to play repeatedly.

What you do

The children stand in pairs opposite each other in an inner and outer circle formation. The dancing is done in time to the music, which has an easy lilt.

(a) Partners hold hands and swing arms from side to side, seven times.

(b) On the 'and eight' count, clap and stamp feet (the recording will make this obvious!).

(c) Pick up hands again with partner and swing arms seven times finishing with a wave and the words 'Bye-bye' as the inner partners move along one place to the left. Start the dance again, this time with a new partner.

(d) Repeat the dance until the children eventually reach the partner they began with.

MOVE ALONG

See the written music in activity number 20, which may clarify these dance instructions for you.

22. Circle Fun

What you need

One large circle of children, sitting on the floor to learn the chant.

What you do

Learn the chant as follows:

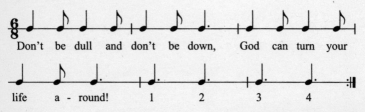

Stand in a circle formation and hold hands. Chant the words, while taking eight steps clockwise. Stand on the spot and at the same speed count aloud, one to four, while doing the following actions:

CIRCLE FUN

1   = clap

2 3 4 = turn on the spot, clockwise

Hold hands once more, repeat the chant and actions, but rotate anticlockwise.

This circle fun can get quite furious, especially if you increase the speed of the chant!

23. Blow the Trumpet, Bang the Drum

Biblical reference

Psalm 150

Prayer

What fun we have praising you in music. Thank you, Lord, for happy songs that we can share together. Amen.

Song words

1. Blow the trumpet,
   Bang the drum.
   Clash the cymbals one by one.
   Twang the strings and stay around –
   We're praising God in glorious sound.

2. Toot-toot, toot-toot,
   Bing-bang-bong.
   Clish-clash, clish-clash,
   Twing-twang-twong!
   Play the music, stay around –
   We're praising God in glorious sound.

Actions

Make appropriate gestures to imitate playing the trumpet, the drum, the cymbals and the guitar.

BLOW THE TRUMPET, BANG THE DRUM
(actions)

24. Big Band March

What you need

An assortment of instruments: see 'How to Use This Book' for ideas.

What you do

The children each hold an instrument, and line up behind a leader. Play the backing track to the song 'Blow the Trumpet, Bang the Drum', programmed to repeat over and over.

March up and down and round and round in single file, playing the instruments. It can be fun to put out some obstacles, like chairs, which the leader must march and weave around. Young children, though, will be happy just to proceed round the room. If the children are nursery age, don't attempt to form a single file – just let them march around at will.

Section 2

How to Live

25. Equipping a Child for Life

Biblical references

Proverbs 22:6

James 1:27

James 2:14–17

Prayer

Dear Lord, thank you for all those who love us and show us right from wrong – our parents, families, teachers and friends. Give us a big heart and a generous nature to share our things with children who are less fortunate than ourselves. Amen.

Song words

> Teach a child in the way he should go
> And when he is old he will not turn away.
> The Bible tells us to care for the fatherless
> And let them share good things.

Chorus (sing through twice)
> Equipping a child for life.
> Equipping a child for life.
> We'll do it now in Jesus' name
> And turn a precious life around.

Please see pages 78–79 for the full music to this song.

This song also has an instrumental melody for kazoos, which can be bought from a toy shop. Alternatively blow thin paper over a comb for the same effect. The instrumental melody can be played on any available suitable melodic instrument, and can be played on its own or over the song tune. Refer to the CD recording for ideas. The addition of a drum kit is ideal.

Melody for kazoos

N.B. This melody can be played with the singing.

EQUIPPING A CHILD FOR LIFE

EQUIPPING A CHILD FOR LIFE

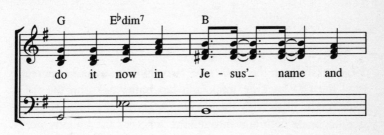

26. Pulse and Rhythm

What you need

Rhythm sticks and a clear floor area: if this is free of carpet, so much the better. The backing track to the song 'Equipping a child for life'.

What you do

Sit in a circle on the floor with two rhythm sticks per person. Play the CD backing track and tap both sticks on the floor together in time with the regular beats of the music. These regular beats continue throughout, whether the melody notes coincide or not. These beats are called the pulse.

Now replay the backing track, but this time tap the two sticks together to coincide with the words, so that the sticks are heard tapping along with the melody. Explain that this is called the rhythm.

When the children are competent at playing both the pulse and the rhythm, divide them into two groups, with one group beating the pulse on the floor, and the other tapping the rhythm. Change the groups around, so that everyone has a go at both pulse and rhythm.

27. Be Not Overcome with Evil

Biblical references

Romans 12:9–21

Proverbs 16:7

Matthew 5:38–46

Prayer

Lord Jesus Christ, help us to overcome the desire to do and say bad things to people who are unkind and hurtful to us. Teach us that it is better to be kind and generous than cruel and mean. Help us to show love to everyone. Amen.

Song words (sing through twice)

> Be not overcome with evil,
> But overcome evil with good.
> Love your enemy,
> Make him a friend,
> And then,
> You'll never need to hate him ever again!

BE NOT OVERCOME WITH EVIL

BE NOT OVERCOME WITH EVIL

28. Good Triumphs over Evil

What you need

A wide selection of school percussion instruments, or other items selected to make a variety of sounds.

What you do

Sit in a circle with the instruments in the centre. Explain that you are looking for sounds to represent 'good' (gentle, warm, bright and sustained sounds). Invite the children to try out some of the instruments and then discuss together whether the sounds are appropriate. Delegate the chosen instruments to particular children.

Now explain that you are looking for sounds to represent 'evil' (harsh, loud, grating, persistent, sinister and discordant sounds). Delegate these instruments to children. It would be good if everyone had something to play.

You conduct as follows:

(a) The 'good' instruments begin softly and rise to a medium level of sound and continue.

(b) The 'evil' instruments join in softly, but gradually get louder and louder until they obliterate the sound of the 'good' instruments.

(c) After a very noisy war of sound, the 'evil' sounds get softer and fade away, leaving the gentle, softer sounds playing on their own.

The 'good' triumphs over the 'evil'!

29. Conversation

What you need

Children to work in pairs. Each child chooses an instrument with a contrasting sound to his or her partner's.

What you do

The instruments 'talk' to each other as if having a conversation:

(a) a pleasant conversation with questions and answers

(b) an argument resolved with both 'saying' sorry

(c) children devise their own conversations

Don't forget that laughter plays an important part in everyday conversations. Try to invent a 'laughing' sound on the instruments.

30. The People of God's Church Are One Body

Biblical references

Ephesians 4:14–16
1 Corinthians 12:12–27

Prayer

Dear Lord, your church is made up of people who know and serve you. It isn't a place or building made with bricks and stones. Help us to understand that just as our bodies are made up of different parts, so your church too is made up of people with varying talents and skills. No one is better or more important than another. Every member of your church is needed in their own special way. Amen.

Song words

The people of God's church are one body,
One body is the church of the Lord.
Each part is not the same,
But is known by its own name.
Yes, the body of the church has many parts.

1. The foot is not the eye,
   And the ear is not the nose.
   And the lips and teeth are nothing like our knees.
   All the workings deep inside
   Are so busy as they hide
   Their necessary life giving work.

   The people of God's church are one body. . . .

2. The wrist is not the back
   And the chin is not the hair.
   And the tongue is nothing like a little toe.
   So you see that different bits
   Are all needed and they knit
   Into a body fit for the Lord!

   The people of God's church are one body. . . .

Actions

Have fun pointing to the various body parts as you sing!

THE PEOPLE OF GOD'S CHURCH ARE ONE BODY
(actions)

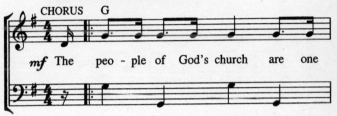

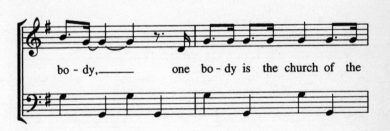

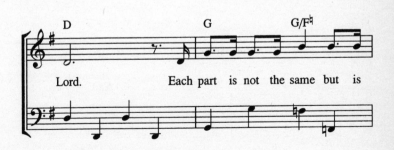

THE PEOPLE OF GOD'S CHURCH ARE ONE BODY

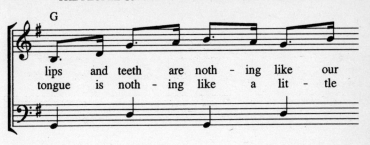

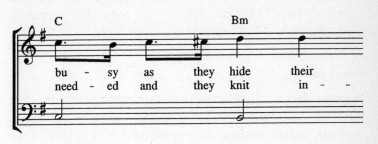
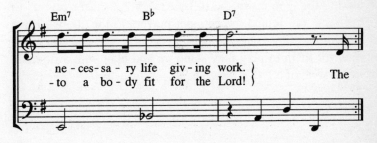

31. Shakers and Tube Trumpets

What you need

All sizes and shapes of shakers and a selection of cardboard tubes (such as are found inside kitchen paper rolls) to play as trumpets. The CD backing track to the song 'The people of God's church'.

What you do

Practise playing along to the recording with shakers. Playing them at shoulder height, as if mixing a South American cocktail, is fun! Practise the cardboard tube trumpets, toot-tooting the tune down the rolls. Assign the shaker players to the verse music and the trumpet players to the chorus. Have fun with seating your trumpet players in a row, and when it is time for them to play they stand up and play with a flourish, in the style of a 1940s dance band.

32. Blowing Bottles

What you need

A collection of empty two-litre, one-litre and half-litre soft drink bottles with narrow necks.

What you do

Ask the children which bottles will produce the deepest sound (the biggest) and which bottles will produce the highest sound (the smallest). Give out the bottles (minus their screw caps) and ask the children to blow across the bottle tops to make a sound akin to a cruise ship leaving port.

Time will be needed to practise getting a good sound. Be prepared for some children to get a little cross when they can't get a note. Others will be delighted to hit on just the right breath control and angle of blowing to produce an excellent sound. (You may care to practise bottle-blowing at home before trying to play in front of other people!)

Once enough practising has been done by the children, play any lively backing track from the CD and blow the bottles at any place.

33. Greed in the End Is No Friend

Biblical references

Proverbs 4:24–27

Proverbs 10:9

Proverbs 12:22

Acts 5:1–11

Prayer

Dear Jesus, help us to be strong enough always to tell the truth, and keep us from being greedy and mean. Amen.

What you do

Practise both parts of the song with all the children together before dividing them into two groups and singing as a song with two parts.

Song words

Part one

> Be honest and true in the things that you do,
> Don't ever try to cover up the truth.
> Remember Ananias who cheated on God!
> Greed in the end is no friend.

Part two

> So tell the truth and don't tell lies,
> Holding back is never wise.
> It's not cool to be a fool!
> Greed in the end is no friend.

GREED IN THE END IS NO FRIEND
(two parts)

GREED IN THE END IS NO FRIEND

Only attempt singing the two parts together once the children are able to sing the song all the way through with confidence.

34. Hitting the Right Pitch

What you need

A selection of chime bars, suitably pitched at voice level. Be careful not to choose bars that are too high.

What you do

Chant the following rhythm using a usual speaking voice:

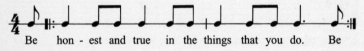

Now choose one chime bar, and play the rhythm on the chime bar and sing the word pattern on the same note. Change the chime bar, and play and sing imitating the pitch of that note. Not everyone (especially the very young) will be able to copy the pitch of the chime bars, but make it fun. For a change, dispense with the chime bars, and say the chant in a high squeaky voice, or in a low, deep voice. This should produce a few laughs!

35. The Gardener Sows His Seed

Biblical references

Isaiah 28:24–29

Matthew 13:31–32

Hebrews 6:7–8

Prayer

Dear Lord, our lives are like a garden. Our talents are lying asleep, like little seeds in winter. Please be our sunshine and our soft warm rain and help us to grow into really useful people for you. Amen.

Song words

1. The gardener sows his seed
   In a place where he can weed.
   And he'll hoe all day and into the night
   To get his garden growing right!

2. The garden is our life,
   Which we'll spend in trouble and strife
   If we let the weeds grow all over the place.
   They'll choke God's love and hide his face.

3. So, work hard every day,
   Throw the trash and weeds away.
   Then the garden of life will be God's delight,
   And everything will turn out right!
   That's right!

THE GARDENER SOWS HIS SEED

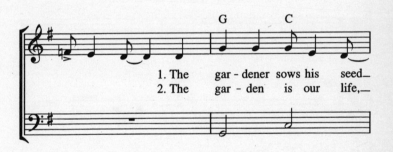

1. The gar-dener sows his seed in a place where he can weed.
2. The gar-den is our life, which we'll spend in trou-ble and strife

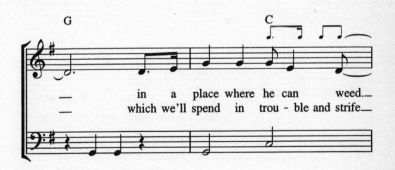

THE GARDENER SOWS HIS SEED

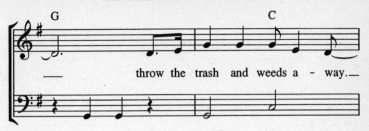
throw the trash and weeds a-way.

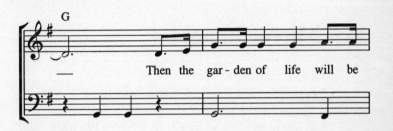
Then the gar-den of life will be

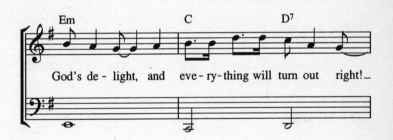
God's de-light, and eve-ry-thing will turn out right!

(whispered) That's right!

36. Mirror Images

What you need

Children in pairs, and the CD backing track to the song 'The gardener sows his seed'.

What you do

The children stand in pairs, face to face. One child will do actions, while the other must be a mirror image. Neither child is allowed to move from their designated spot. The actions could include:

(a) casting of seed

(b) hoeing

(c) growing

(d) being a plant waving in the wind

(e) cutting with garden shears

Change the 'acting' and the 'mirror' children around.

37. Growing Plants

What you need

A single suspended cymbal and two soft beaters.

What you do

The children crouch on the floor making themselves as small as possible, with arms and legs tucked in. The cymbal is played with gentle, quiet strokes, and the children gradually begin to grow. The cymbal roll gets louder and louder, and faster and faster as the children grow into fully formed plants. Give an enormous cymbal crash to indicate that the children must 'freeze' their position. This should be their biggest, widest and tallest position as a fully grown plant or tree.

Count to ten as these positions are held. On the count of ten, crash the cymbal again and the children suddenly and like lightning crouch down again in their starting positions as a seed. Repeat this several times. You may find it helpful to vocally encourage the children by saying, 'Grow . . . grow . . . grow . . . grow . . . STOP!'

38. Scatter Seeds of Good Today

Biblical references

Ecclesiastes 11:4–6

Galatians 6:9

Prayer

Dear God, unless we sow a seed we will never grow a plant. If we never sow seeds of good, we'll never reap a bumper harvest for you. What can we do today to bring your harvest a little bit nearer? Amen.

Song words

> *If you want to reap the harvest,*
> *First learn how to sow.*
> *Scatter seeds of good today.*
> *Seeds can be our thoughts of others,*
> *Things we do and say.*
> *Scatter seeds of good today.*

SCATTER SEEDS OF GOOD TODAY

1. Jesus taught us how to pray,
   How to live our lives each day.
   Scatter seeds of good today.

   If you want to reap the harvest....

2. Learn from Jesus how to live,
   How to make your harvest big.
   Scatter seeds of good today.

   If you wish to reap the harvest....

SCATTER SEEDS OF GOOD TODAY

SCATTER SEEDS OF GOOD TODAY

39. Heel and Toe

What you need

The CD backing track to the song 'If you wish to reap the harvest'.

What you do

(a) Stand on the spot and, using one foot, point repeatedly with heel then toes, to words 'heel-toe, heel-toe, heel-toe . . .' in time with the music. Repeat with the other foot. (Some children will attempt both feet together!)

(b) Taking steps in time to the music, walk like this:

on tip toes

on heels

with straight backs and bent knees!

40. Don't Be a Copycat of Things That Are Bad

Biblical references

Philippians 4:8–9

Proverbs 3:31

Proverbs 26:4

Prayer

Dear Lord of all creation, help us only to copy things that are good, and to say 'no' to bad things. Help us not to feel unsure or silly in front of other people if we do have to say 'no'. Amen.

Song words

Don't be a copycat of things that are bad,
You would be mad to copy the bad.
Just be a copycat of things that are good,
Then you'll live your life like you really should.

Don't be a copycat of things that are bad,
You would be mad to copy the bad.
Say 'hello' to the things that are right,
'Bye-bye bad. Get out of our sight!'

Just copy, copy all the things that are good.
Copy, copy, copy, copy, copy, copy, copy, copy.
Copy the things that are good. YEAH!

(The children may find it helpful to use their fingers to count off the nine 'copy's'.)

DON'T BE A COPYCAT
OF THINGS THAT ARE BAD

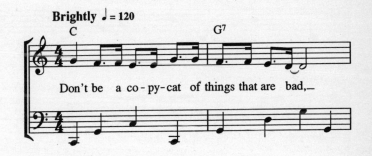

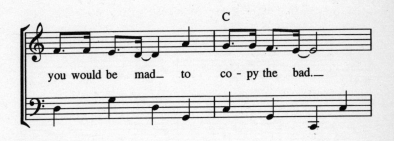

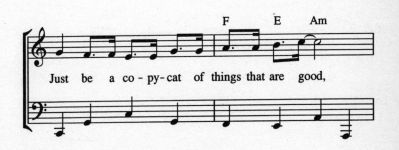

DON'T BE A COPYCAT OF THINGS THAT ARE BAD

"Bye - bye bad. Get out of our sight!"
Just co - py, co - py all the things that are good.
*Co - py, co - py, co - py, co - py, co - py, co - py, co - py, co - py.
Co - py the things that are good.— YEAH!

* Children can count out the next nine 'copy's' on fingers!

41. Follow My Sticks

What you need

Rhythm sticks and the backing track to the song 'Don't be a copycat of things that are bad'.

What you do

Practise clapping gently to the beats on the recording, counting '1 2 3 4'. Everyone has two rhythm sticks and sits in a circle on the floor. The children must follow the leader, and everything must be done to the beats of the music, as just practised.

Vary the way the sticks are played as follows:

(a) Tap both sticks together (replaces hand claps).

(b) Tap both sticks at the same time on the floor.

(c) Tap the sticks on the floor, but alternately (right, left, right, left, etc.).

42. Copy My Guiro Rhythm

What you need

Guiros or home-made substitutes.

What you do

The children work in pairs and each child has a guiro. One child is the leader and scrapes a short pattern on his guiro. The partner makes an exact copy on his guiro. So begins a copycat interlude.

Encourage the children to keep things simple at first. Older and more able children may develop some quite complicated rhythms. If you are working with very young children, have them sit together at your feet, and copy your rhythm. Working in pairs can come later.

43. Gently Rock

Biblical references

Luke 18:15–16

Mark 10:13–16

Prayer

Dear Jesus, you were a baby once. Help us to be tender and loving to all little babies and to be kind to our little brothers and sisters. Amen.

Song words

> Gently rock the little baby to and fro.
> Go to sleep and rest in Jesus, his love flows.
>
> Jesus loves all little children, this is true.
> Everyone finds rest in Jesus, babies too!

Actions

Gently rock arms in front of chest, as if rocking a baby to sleep. If children are very young, they could gently rock a doll or favourite cuddly toy.

GENTLY ROCK
(actions)

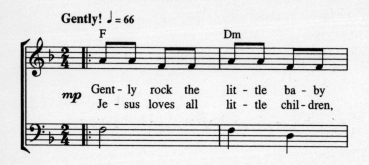

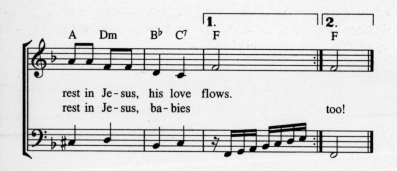

44. Sharing Favourite Toys

What you need

A favourite cuddly toy brought in by each child. The CD backing track to the song 'Gently rock'.

What you do

The children sit in a circle, and sing the song 'Gently rock', while rocking their favourite toy. When the song is finished, each child passes his or her favourite toy clockwise to the next child, ready to sing the song again, but this time with a toy that isn't theirs. Continue in the same manner until the children get their favourite toy back again. Welcome the special toy back with a big hug!

45. Out of the Boat

Biblical reference

Genesis 8:16–18

What you need

A referee's whistle; a selection of xylophones, glockenspiels, metallophones and chime bars, and a soft beater for each player. Alternatively use anything which makes a rocking sound, whether a traditional musical instrument or not. Only half (or fewer) children have an instrument to play.

What you do

Say the following words as the children with instruments run the beaters lightly up and down the instruments producing a rocking motion:

'Rock, rock, to and fro.
Out of the boat you must go!'

The whistle is then given a sharp blast, and the children who have instruments stop playing and pass the instruments to those children who were without. They now have a turn, until the next blast on the whistle, when it will be 'all change' again.

To tease the children, extend the rhyme, at will, by repeating the first line, so keeping them in anticipation of when the boat will be 'tipped' up by the whistle blast.

'Rock, rock, to and fro.
Rock, rock, to and fro.
Rock, rock, to and fro . . .
Out of the boat you must go!'

46. Humpty-Dumpty Was a Duff Egg

Biblical reference

Ecclesiastes 4:10

Prayer

Dear Lord, keep us in a place of safety, where we have our feet firmly on the ground and planted in your ways. Keep us from climbing, wobbling and falling. Amen.

Song words

Humpty-Dumpty was a duff egg,
He didn't stay down,
But climbed up instead.
Smashed into pieces,
He took a big fall.
What a duff egg to climb up the wall!

Actions

The children sit on a low bench, which is Humpty's wall. At the end of the song all the children tumble off the wall onto the floor. Get back onto the bench as quickly as possible, ready to repeat the song.

HUMPTY-DUMPTY WAS A DUFF EGG
(actions)

47. Smash!

Biblical reference

Ecclesiastes 4:10

What you need

A double-sided card with a picture of Humpty-Dumpty on one side, and on the reverse, a shape to signify 'smash!'. Enough percussion instruments for everyone.

What you do

Hold up the picture of Humpty-Dumpty, and say all together 'Humpty-Dumpty' for as long as his picture is showing. As soon as you reverse the card and show the 'smash!' sign, the children play their instruments. They stop playing when you reverse the card and once again show Humpty's picture. Vary the length of time between reversing the card.

48. Mugs and Cups

What you need

Some sturdy mugs and cups (definitely not from the best tea set!) and teaspoons. The backing track to the song 'Humpty-Dumpty was a duff egg'.

What you do

Give each child a mug or cup and a teaspoon. Play the music and at the words 'Smashed into pieces . . .' tinkle the spoons in the mugs and cups as loudly as possible. No child should play his mug or cup until the right words are reached. Resisting the temptation to play while waiting with spoon in hand is hard to do when you are small! You may have to call 'stop' when you are ready to repeat the song.

49. Little Bo-Peep Had Silly Sheep

Biblical references

John 10:1–5

Psalm 119:176

Prayer

Dear God, we know you love us all and know us by our name. If we keep looking and listening for you, we can't get lost. Amen.

Song words

> Little Bo-Peep had silly sheep
> Who went for a walk on their own.
> They were not known
> Away from their home.
> Thank goodness they heard her voice calling.

LITTLE BO-PEEP
HAD SILLY SHEEP

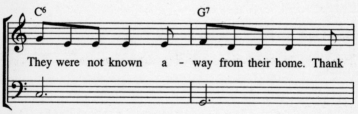
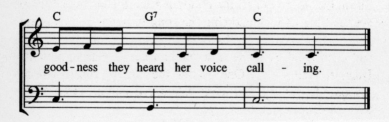

50. Shepherd's Name-calling Game

Biblical references

Psalm 23:1

John 10:14

What you need

The song 'Little Bo-Peep had silly sheep', and an assistant.

What you do

Sit on the floor with all the children around you (the children are the little lambs), and sing the song through. The assistant gets up and leads the lambs away to a corner of the room. You call each child by name in a gentle voice – 'Susan, Sancha, Damian, Harry, etc.'. One by one the 'lambs' run to you in response to hearing their name called. All snuggle close ready to begin the song all over again.

Index of Themes

The following index is not exhaustive and you will probably discover other theme links for yourself. Numbers refer to activities not pages.

Bullies	6
Change	10, 22
Church	30, 31
Creation	3, 4, 35, 36, 37, 38
Disappointment	6
Faith	5, 10, 12, 14, 17, 20
Fear	5, 20, 49
Forgiveness	6, 12
Giving	25, 26, 27, 38
Good and evil	28, 29, 35, 38, 40, 41
Greed	33, 44, 45
Harvest	37, 38, 39
Help	7
Jesus as King	2
Lord's Prayer, The	1
Love	11, 12, 14, 16, 17, 18, 19, 27
Names	49, 50
Praise	23, 24
Pride	46

INDEX OF THEMES

Thirst	13
Trinity	8, 9
Worry	20, 21, 43

Resources

The Way – Christian's Path to Happiness An exciting children's musical based on John Bunyan's *The Pilgrim's Progress*, with words and music by Alison Hedger. Music book and CD   AH00800 (includes production notes and background information). Pupil's play part   AH00900. Available from Golden Apple Productions.

For further information

A wide selection of music suitable for school and Sunday schools, much of it written, arranged and edited by Alison Hedger, is available from Golden Apple Productions. A comprehensive catalogue is available on request from:

Music Sales Limited
The Distribution Centre
Newmarket Road
Bury St Edmunds
Suffolk IP33 3YB
www.musicroom.com

CD Track List

Item number in book	With singing	Without singing
1. Father in heaven	1	21
3. My eyes have seen the glory of the Lord	2	22
5. Be still and know that I am God	3	23
8. Three in One	4	24
10. Jesus will be the same today (two parts)	5	25
12. Nothing can separate us from God's love (a round)	6	26
14. Love the Lord with all of your heart	7	27
17. Jesus loves me (actions)	8	28
20. Take all your troubles to Jesus*	9	29*
23. Blow the trumpet, bang the drum (actions)	10	30
25. Equipping a child for life (melody for kazoos)	11	31
27. Be not overcome with evil	12	32

CD TRACK LIST

30. The people of God's church are one body (actions)	13	33
33. Greed in the end is no friend (two parts)	14	34
35. The gardener sows his seed	15	35
38. Scatter seeds of good today	16	36
40. Don't be a copycat of things that are bad	17	37
43. Gently rock (actions)	18	38
46. Humpty-Dumpty was a duff egg	19	39
49. Little Bo-Peep had silly sheep	20	40

***Bonus track number 41** for uninterrupted dancing to 'Take all your troubles to Jesus'.

Children's Ministry Teaching Programme

- Do you want to see children develop a personal relationship with Jesus?

- Do you want teaching sessions that are fun, biblical, evangelical and interactive?

- Would you like children to enjoy age-appropriate activities as they learn about God?

If you've said YES to any of these questions, you need the Children's Ministry Teaching Programme.

The Children's Ministry Teaching Programme provides four leader's guides covering ages from under 3 to 13+; KidZone activity books for children aged 5-7, 7-9 and 9-11; MiniKidz and KidZone craft books for children aged 3-5 and 5-9, a magazine for those over 11; a CD of music and stories; and FamilyZone with song words, ideas for all-age worship and parents' letters.

**For more information visit our web site
www.childrensministry.co.uk**

100 Worship Activities for Children

by Chris Leach

This practical resource gives ideas for activities and games that illustrate the true meaning of worship, to help lead children into a deeper relationship with God.

Many are also suitable for all-age services, designed to bring new life and exuberance to your church's worship time.

The ideas are listed under seasons of the church year, with full theme and Scripture indexes.

100 Creative Prayer Ideas for Children

by Jan Dyer

Children are made in the image of a Creator God, and they enjoy being creative themselves! So it makes sense to use a variety of ways to stimulate children to develop their prayer lives. That way they can build a meaningful friendship with him that will last a lifetime.

Jan Dyer has provided an array of tried and tested ideas, divided into ten areas of a child's life:

- family life
- school life
- friends
- my neighbourhood
- my country
- the world
- myself
- creation
- God's work
- God's word

100 Simple Bible Craft Ideas for Children

by Sue Price

Many of us learn more effectively when we have something to see and something to make; when we can interact rather than simply sit and listen. Crafts can therefore be used as a vital part of any session with children, and not just an add-on.

This collection of illustrated ideas has been specifically designed to help children learn stories and truths from the Bible in such a way that they can make them part of their lives. They are ideal for teachers who would not regard themselves as experts, yet can easily be adapted by the more experienced!

The ideas have been grouped according to categories:
- Bible stories
- lesson reminders
- aids to worship
- crafts to give
- seasonal items

The result is a ready-to-use collection that will prove invaluable to anyone who plays a part in the teaching of children.